FOOD STORAGE 101 WHERE DO I BEGIN?

To obtain extra copies of this and other books on the subject of food storage, see order form in the back of this book or call the phone number below. Wholesale & quantity discounts are available for stores, churches and other groups.

Peggy Layton
P.O. Box 44
Manti, Utah 84642
435-835-0311
Fax: 435-851-0777
E-mail splayton@sisna.com
www.peggylayton.net

Table Of Contents

Noah's Ark. 5
Prepare Your Own Personal Home
    Grocery Store and Pharmacy 7
Food In The Basement Is Better Than
    Money In The Bank. 7
A Three Month Well Rounded
    Food Storage Plan 13
Six Step Plan of Action 14
Six Steps To Family Preparedness. 15
Step One First Priority. 24
Location For Your Home Grocery Store 24
Shelves and Storage Areas. 26
Alternative Cooking and Other
    Equipment Needed 35
Water for Emergencies 35
Water Storage 36
Water Purification. 38
Special Diets and Medications 40
Step Two The Basic Ingredients for Baking . 40
Baby Food 40
Steps Three, Four, and Five 42
What To Store and How Much To Store. 42
Grains 42
Legumes. 42
Milk And Dairy Products 43
Sweeteners 43
Fruits. 43
Vegetables 43

Fats And Oils. 43
Meats And Meat Substitutes 44
Sprouting Seeds And Beans 44
Gardening Seeds 44
Flavorings And Adjunct Food 45
Psychological Foods. 45
How Much Food Do I Need For One-year?. . . 45
Chart: Suggested Amounts To Store 46
What To Store And How Much To Store 46
How To Store Bulk Foods 47
Storage Containers 47
5 or 6 Gallon Buckets or Pails 47
10 Size Double Enamel Cans 48
Mylar Bags 48
Oxygen Absorber Packets 49
Dry Ice Method 49
Co2 or Nitrogen Flush Method. 49
Bay Leaves Method. 50
Freezing Grain Method. 50
Diatomaceous Earth Method 50
The Causes of Deterioration. 51
Oxygen. 51
Bacteria 51
Insects 51
Shelf Life 52
Light 52
Temperature 53
Humidity and Moisture 53
Location 53
Dehydrated Foods 53
Reconstituting Guidelines 55

Reconstituting Chart 56
Step Six Non food Items 57
Menu Planning 58
Two Week Menu Planning Chart 58
Charts 60
Itemized Weekly Ingredients 74
Rotation of Foods 76
Inventory and Planning Guide 77
Planning Your Food Storage Program 77
Instructions 78
Inventory and Planning Chart for a Basic
        And Balanced Food Storage Plan 81

Noah's Ark

"Behold, what is he doing?
That man there in his yard?
He's hammering and sawing,
he's working very hard."

"Oh, yes, of course, you're new here.
That's Noah, he says thus.
Repent! The Lord commands it!
Or else he'll destroy us!"

"He says a flood is coming.
He's been raving on for years.
But nothing yet has happened,
so you need have no more fears."

"You mean he builds a boat there,
working until night,
to save him from disaster,
well, what if he is right?"

"Oh, no, don't you start that now!
People might say you're sick,
if you begin agreeing with
that raving lunatic!"

And so the people gossiped,
yelling rude and unkind words.
But Noah worked on steadily,
because he never heard.

At last the ark was finished,
then the crowd began to jeer.
"What will you do now sir,
there is no water near?"

Yet Noah kept on working,
with his wife, in-laws and sons,
to put food in the ark now,
hay, seed, and grain by the tons.

Then animals were gathered,
brought to the ark's front door.
Came jeers of, "when ya cruising?
What are the critters for?"

When Noah at last finished,
the light was getting dim,
he turned and said, "will you repent?"
The crowd threw rocks at him.

So Noah took his family,
into the food filled ark.
He closed the door, the rain began,
the sky was fully dark.

The ark had been for years now,
a joke for all the town.
It floated up and off, away,
and all the jeerers drowned.

Author
Shirley Bahlman

PREPARE YOUR OWN PERSONAL HOME GROCERY STORE AND PHARMACY

"Food in the basement is better than money in the bank."

There are many reasons for stockpiling a one-year supply of food. The value of food commodities generally increases at the same rate as inflation. Money in the bank doesn't do that. Investing in five hundred cans of tuna fish in your basement is a better bet than putting $350.00 in the bank.

The most important reason to store food is that it comes in very handy in a crisis of any kind. Whether it be a large emergency such as an earthquake, flood, volcano eruption, war, strike, economic crash, or as personal as being laid off work, moving, helping other family members that are down and out or when cash is short. It is comforting to know that you can use your home grocery store to help buffer lean money times. If you had to live on what you had in your basement for an extended period of time, you would wish you had a well-rounded supply of food.

For forty years the leader of a prominent church in Utah has been encouraging its members to store a one-year supply of food, water, clothing and fuel. The practice has paid off many times. One example is when the Teton Dam broke in Eastern Idaho and swept through several small farming communities.

7

The church members living on higher ground used their personal food supplies to feed the homeless.

There were layoffs in large companies, which left 6,000 employers without paychecks. Many had food in their homes to carry them through the three months with out work.

Natural Disasters are happening more frequently now. The hurricanes and earthquakes take their toll on lives and leave people homeless and without food. The more recent natural disaster in Honduras took its toll. Over 8,000 people were left homeless. The communities rallied and helped dig each other out. Cargo planes full of food and provisions were flown in to help the people. Without this extra food and help, these people would have starved to death.

In general, most households do not have more than a 1-week supply of food. "Let's face it, as a nation, we rely almost totally on the supermarket and fast food restaurants." An average family of four spends $550.00 or more per month on food. As the children grow up, the price increases. That is double the amount spent ten years ago. In the past five years inflation on food has risen more than anything else has. Your best investment right now is FOOD!

If you ask any supermarket chain manager to tell you how long it would take to empty the shelves in any store in the event of a crises, the answer would be approximately three days. They just don't keep that much in their warehouses. And if there were a trucking problem it would be less. People would storm the grocery stores and buy anything they could get. The water is the first thing that goes.

I strongly suggest that you find a place in your home, either in a basement, spare bedroom, closet, junk room, under the stairway or heated garage, and go to work fixing it up into your own home grocery store and pharmacy. Somehow get shelves in there, build them, have them built or buy them pre built. "Whatever works" Just do it now!

This "home grocery store" will be to you and your family as the ark was to Noah and his family. It will contain all the necessary food, water, bedding and medical supplies to sustain life for a minimum of three months to one year.

So what are the best kinds of food to stock pile? It is recommended that you "store what you eat and eat what you store" otherwise you might get sick. A crisis is not the time to change your families' diet.

Appetite fatigue is a very serious condition. Food storage experiments have been conducted where people had mock disasters and lived on their food storage for extended periods of time.

In one experiment a family ate nothing but items from their basement stockpile, mostly dehydrated food. Within two weeks there were three members of the family sick and one ended up in the hospital.

If you are suddenly thrown into a diet that you are not use to, especially wheat, beans, corn, honey, powdered milk and dehydrated food, you will have a double crises. One thing we do not need in an emergency is a sickness caused by a drastic change in our diet.

There is nothing wrong with storing wheat, and honey, if that is what you are use to and like it. Some people have allergies to wheat and they find this out when they change their diet. Store a variety of wheat and other grains. Flour, oatmeal, rice, noodles, evaporated milk, beans, peas, lentils, legumes, canned meats, tuna fish, canned salmon, soup of all kinds, tomatoes, sauces of all kinds, all baking items, shortening, oils, peanut butter, jams, syrups, salad dressings, mayonnaise, jello, cocoa, bottled fruits and vegetables, and many other dehydrated products.

Nothing should be kept for more than a year without rotating except the following: wheat, grains, beans, sugar, salt, and any product that is nitrogen packed for long term storage, that has a low oxygen content.

If people eat what they store and store what they eat, the rotation will automatically take care of itself. Rotating your food so your family gets use to eating the grains, beans, honey and dehydrated products is very important

Always replace each item as it is used up so you can maintain your stockpile. Purchase cases of items when they come on sale. Our hometown grocery store has case lot sales about four times a year. The best prices are when items are in season. I buy wet pack corn and beans in the fall when they are two cans for $1.00. When tuna fish comes on sale I buy five or six cases. It's an excellent source of protein and I save a lot of money by purchasing in bulk.

A sample formula for knowing how much food to store is to keep track of what you eat for a two-week period of time. Surprisingly most families repeat meals every few days. Multiply the basic ingredients by six to calculate a three month supply, thirteen for a six month supply and twenty six to calculate a years supply. Separate menus can be calculated for summer and winter taking into consideration gardening and seasonal foods available. Build your own stockpile slowly, over a six-month period of time.

A hint that has helped me to obtain extra food items, is that every time I go to the grocery store, I get two of each item that I normally buy, such as ketchup, barbecue sauce, pickles, olives, cream soups, mayonnaise, salad dressing, spaghetti sauces, mixes, etc. I put one away and use the other. It's a good idea to keep adding more and more of a variety of items to your home grocery store, so your diet won't be so bland.

Planned menus can eliminate the panic feeling you get when you know you should store food and you don't know where to begin.

I have included a chart in this book for you to plan your own menus for two weeks. Be sure to list every ingredient to make sure you have each item on hand.

If you plan your food storage program out carefully you can avoid impulse or panic buying which will save you a lot of money and grief.

Anticipate your needs for a three-month period of time. Buy bulk food in larger quantities and store them in plastic food grade buckets that have airtight lids. Do not use paint buckets or any other container that has been used for chemicals. Do not use garbage bags, they are treated with pesticides. A food grade mylar liner inside a plastic bucket works very well with an oxygen absorber vacuum packed and sealed.

A #10 (1 gallon) can is the best way to store smaller quantities. We will be discussing the different methods of storing bulk food later in this chapter. Store your food in a cool, dry place away from sunlight and in a place that stays a constant temperature of around 40-60 degrees F. Hot or cold fluctuations in temperatures can destroy the nutritive value of the food and shorten the shelf life.

Always label every can, bottle or bucket with, what is in each container, the dates of purchase, shelf life, and the date to be used by.

Most churches have canning equipment that they let their members use. They will allow you to sign up to use the church cannery. You buy your food in bulk and can it yourself in #10 size cans (1 gallon) with the oxygen absorbers. The church will sell you all the supplies needed. You use their equipment to nitrogen pack and seal your cans, label them, and store them. Six cans fit in a box and the boxes stack well on top of each other. It's a very economical way to get food storage

There are food storage groups getting together and canning food. The canning equipment can be purchased along with the #10 size cans and oxygen absorbers and other necessary items. If you need this information please call me.

A Three Month Well Rounded Food Storage Plan

A three-month well-rounded supply of food storage is much better than a year's supply of wheat, beans, honey and powdered milk. The basics are important, but it is just the beginning.

I have divided this plan of action into six steps. Each month you work on one step and after six months you will have a "three month or more" supply of food storage, vitamins, minerals, clothing, bedding, fuel, medical supplies and non-food items to sustain your family in a crises.

Obtaining a years supply of these items is an overwhelming project, so do it in stages. Get a three-month supply of food. After you have completed a three-month supply of food, move on to do it all over again, get a six month, then a nine month, then a years supply.

Noah preached that, every family needed their own boat. They didn't listen and thought the church or government would miraculously save them. It didn't happen. "Pay attention"! We need to listen. Every family needs their own grocery store. Within six months you can be prepared. Just follow this six-step program. Do it smart with a plan. But most of all just "DO IT"!

Plan of Action

A (6 STEP) PLAN OF ACTION

STEP 1:
Clean Out A Room
Prepare Shelves For Your
    Home Grocery Store And
    Pharmacy
Alternative Cooking Methods
Garden Seeds
Water Storage
Mandatory Medications

STEP 2:
Basics For Baking
Baby Food

STEP 3:
Grains
Beans
Legumes
Cereals
Pastas
Spices
Sprouting Seeds
Commercial Soups
Dehydrated Soups
Sauces & Spice Mixes

STEP 4:
Protein Foods
Meat Substitutes
Eggs
Peanut Butter
Psychological Foods

STEP 5:
Commercial Canned
    Fruits
Dehydrated Fruits
Commercial Canned
    Vegetables
Dehydrated Vegetables
Dry Dairy Products
Home Canning

STEP 6:
Non Food Items
Cleansers
Personal Hygiene
Medical Supplies
Personalized Family
    Pharmacy
Personal Medications
Vitamins And Minerals

Six Steps to Family Preparedness

"Store what you eat, eat what you store" Rotate food by using it, replace all food used.

Step #1: Home Grocery Store

Prepare a room in your home

Alternative Cooking Methods and Additional Equipment

Build Shelves & Organize

Instructional Books & Garden Seeds

Garden Seeds
Sweet Corn
Garden Peas
Summer Squash
Banana Squash
Cucumbers
Beets
Carrots
Cabbage
Celery
Onions
Potatoes
Tomatoes
Spinach

Other Instructional Books
Cookin' with Dehydrated Foods
Cookin' with Home Storage
Cookin' with Powdered Milk
Cookin' with Rice & Beans
Cookin' with Wheat & Other Grains

Food Equipment
Juicer
Canning Equipment
Vacuum Sealer
Jars, Lids, Rings, etc.
Water Bath Canner
Pressure Cooker
Bucket Openers
Blender
Mixer

Basic Survival
Dutch Ovens
Propane Cook Stove
Extra Propane
Wood Burning Stove
3 Month Supply of Wood
Metal Grate/Screen for Fire
Matches (12 Boxes)
Electric Grain Mill
Hand Grain Mill
Water Containers
Water Purifier
Buckets & Lids
Sprouting Equipment
Dehydrator

Medications
Anything you cannot live without for 3 months

Water
1 Gallon per person per day (minimum of 3 months supply)

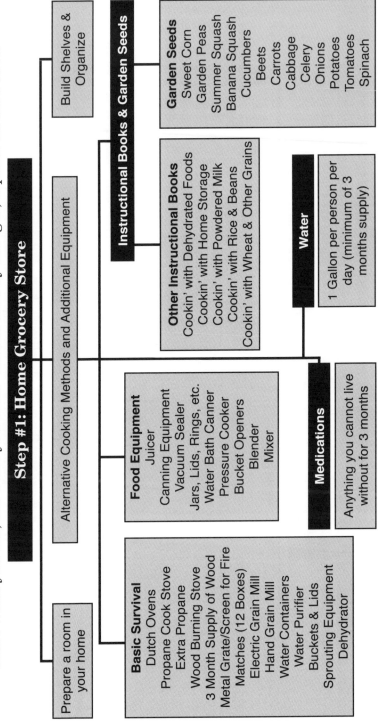

15

Six Steps to Family Preparedness

"Store what you eat, eat what you store" Rotate food by using it, replace all food used.

Step #2: Basic Baking Items & Baby Supplies

Basic Baking Items
Wheat For Grinding*
White Flour*
Powdered Milk*
Dried Whole Egg*
Baking Soda*
Salt*
Baking Powder*
Corn Starch
Yeast

Sweeteners
White Sugar*
Brown Sugar*
Powdered Sugar*
Honey
Molasses
Corn Syrup
Maple Syrup

Fats
Shortening
Olive Oil
Powdered Butter*
Powdered Margarine*
Shortening Powder*

Spices & Flavorings
Cocoa
Cinnamon
Nutmeg
Vanilla
Powdered Lemon

Other Baking Items
Oats*
Cornmeal*
Buttermilk Powder*
Dried Fruit*
Apple Sauce*
Apple Slices*
Bananas*
Fruit Blend*
Raisins*
Chocolate Chips

Baby Supplies
(if applicable)
Baby Food
Formula
Baby Cereal
Evaporated Milk
Karo Syrup
Canned Baby Food
Diapers & Pins
Baby Wipes
Rash Ointment
Baby Bath
Lotion
Shampoo
Baby Medication

* Indicates availability in a #10 metal Can
(approx. 1 gallon)

Six Steps to Family Preparedness

"Store what you eat, eat what you store" Rotate food by using it, replace all food used.

Step #3: Basic Staples

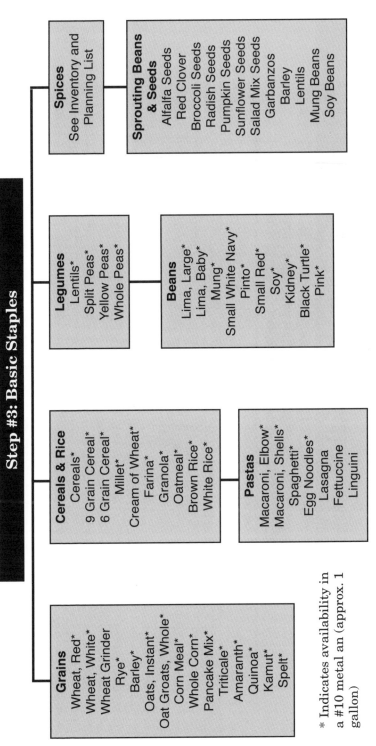

Grains
Wheat, Red*
Wheat, White*
Wheat Grinder
Rye*
Barley*
Oats, Instant*
Oat Groats, Whole*
Corn Meal*
Whole Corn*
Pancake Mix*
Triticale*
Amaranth
Quinoa*
Kamut*
Spelt*

Cereals & Rice
Cereals*
9 Grain Cereal*
6 Grain Cereal*
Millet*
Cream of Wheat*
Farina*
Granola*
Oatmeal*
Brown Rice*
White Rice*

Pastas
Macaroni, Elbow*
Macaroni, Shells*
Spaghetti*
Egg Noodles*
Lasagna
Fettuccine
Linguini

Legumes
Lentils*
Split Peas*
Yellow Peas*
Whole Peas*

Beans
Lima, Large*
Lima, Baby*
Mung*
Small White Navy*
Pinto*
Small Red*
Soy*
Kidney*
Black Turtle*
Pink*

Spices
See Inventory and
Planning List

**Sprouting Beans
& Seeds**
Alfalfa Seeds
Red Clover
Broccoli Seeds
Radish Seeds
Pumpkin Seeds
Sunflower Seeds
Salad Mix Seeds
Garbanzos
Barley
Lentils
Mung Beans
Soy Beans

* Indicates availability in
a #10 metal an (approx. 1
gallon)

17

Six Steps to Family Preparedness

"Store what you eat, eat what you store" Rotate food by using it, replace all food used.

Step #4: Protein Foods

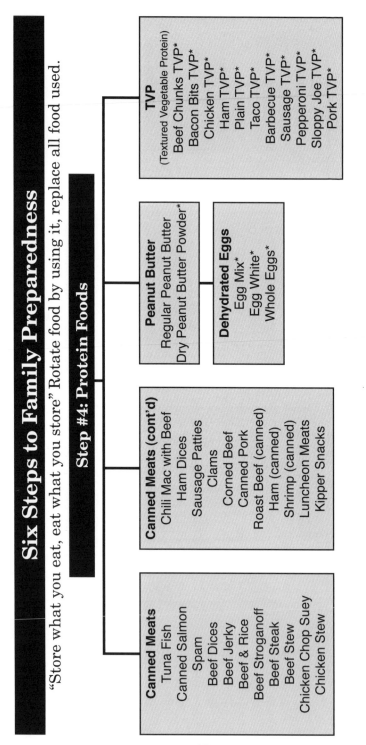

Canned Meats
Tuna Fish
Canned Salmon
Spam
Beef Dices
Beef Jerky
Beef & Rice
Beef Stroganoff
Beef Steak
Beef Stew
Chicken Chop Suey
Chicken Stew

Canned Meats (cont'd)
Chili Mac with Beef
Ham Dices
Sausage Patties
Clams
Corned Beef
Canned Pork
Roast Beef (canned)
Ham (canned)
Shrimp (canned)
Luncheon Meats
Kipper Snacks

Peanut Butter
Regular Peanut Butter
Dry Peanut Butter Powder*

Dehydrated Eggs
Egg Mix*
Egg White*
Whole Eggs*

TVP
(Textured Vegetable Protein)
Beef Chunks TVP*
Bacon Bits TVP*
Chicken TVP*
Ham TVP*
Plain TVP*
Taco TVP*
Barbecue TVP*
Sausage TVP*
Pepperoni TVP*
Sloppy Joe TVP*
Pork TVP*

* Indicates availability in a #10 metal Can (approx. 1 gallon)

Six Steps to Family Preparedness

"Store what you eat, eat what you store" Rotate food by using it, replace all food used.

Step #4: Soups, Sauces & Spice Mixes

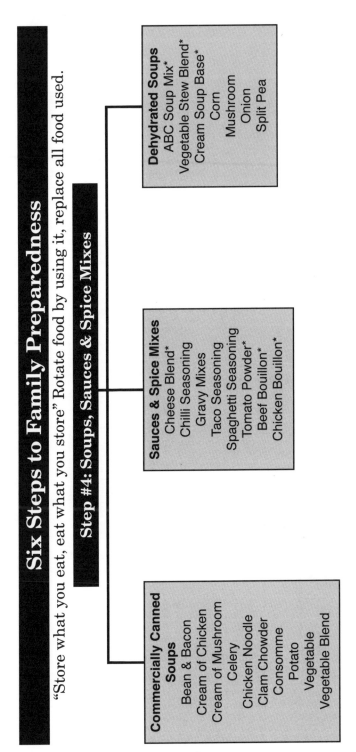

Dehydrated Soups
ABC Soup Mix*
Vegetable Stew Blend*
Cream Soup Base*
Corn
Mushroom
Onion
Split Pea

Sauces & Spice Mixes
Cheese Blend*
Chilli Seasoning
Gravy Mixes
Taco Seasoning
Spaghetti Seasoning
Tomato Powder*
Beef Bouillon*
Chicken Bouillon*

Commercially Canned Soups
Bean & Bacon
Cream of Chicken
Cream of Mushroom
Celery
Chicken Noodle
Clam Chowder
Consomme
Potato
Vegetable
Vegetable Blend

* Indicates availability in a #10 metal Can (approx. 1 gallon)

Six Steps to Family Preparedness

"Store what you eat, eat what you store" Rotate food by using it, replace all food used.

Step #4: Psychological Foods or "Fun Foods"

Drinks
Hot Chocolate Mix*
Lemonade*
Orange Drink Mix*
Tropical Punch*

Desserts
Gelatin, all flavors*
Puddings*
Tapioca
Dessert Fillings
Popcorn*
Jams
Jellies

Boxed Mixes
Cake Mixes
Frosting Mixes
Hamburger Helper
Rice-A-Roni
Bisquick

Canned Drinks
Apple Juice
Apricot Juice
Carrot Juice
Lemonade
Orange Juice
Pineapple Juice
Tomato Juice

Condiments
Ketchup
Mayonnaise
Mustard
Salad Dressing
Hot Peppers
Dill Pickles
Olives
Relish
Sauces
Barbecue Sauce
Soy Sauce
Teriyaki Sauce
Salsa

* Indicates availability in a #10 metal Can (approx. 1 gallon)

Six Steps to Family Preparedness

"Store what you eat, eat what you store." Rotate food by using it, replace all food used.

Step #5: Commercial Fruits & Vegetables

Commercially Canned Fruits
Applesauce
Apple Pie Filling
Apricots
Blueberries
Cherries
Cherry Pie Filling
Fruit Cocktail
Mandarin Oranges
Peaches
Pears
Pineapple
Plums

Dehydrated Fruits
Apple Slices*
Apple Sauce*
Apricots
Banana Slices*
Fruit Blend*
Peach/Apple Flakes*
Strawberry/Apple Flakes*
Prunes
Raisins*
Dates
Figs

Commercially Canned Beans & Vegetables
Asparagus
Beans, Green
Beans, Kidney
Beans, Pinto
Pork and Beans
Carrots
Corn, Whole
Corn, Creamed
Mushrooms
Peas, Sweet Garden
Potatoes
Tomatoes, Stewed
Tomatoes, Whole

Dehydrated Vegetables
Bell Peppers*
Broccoli Florettes*
Carrot Dices*
Cabbage*
Celery*
Onions, Chopped*
Mushrooms, Dried*
Peas, Sweet*
Green Beans*
Corn, Sweet Kernel*
Vegetable Stew*
Tomato Powder*
Potato Dices*
Potato Flakes*
Potato Granules*
Potato Pearls*

Six Steps to Family Preparedness

"Store what you eat, eat what you store" Rotate food by using it, replace all food used.

Step #5: Dried Dairy & Home Canning

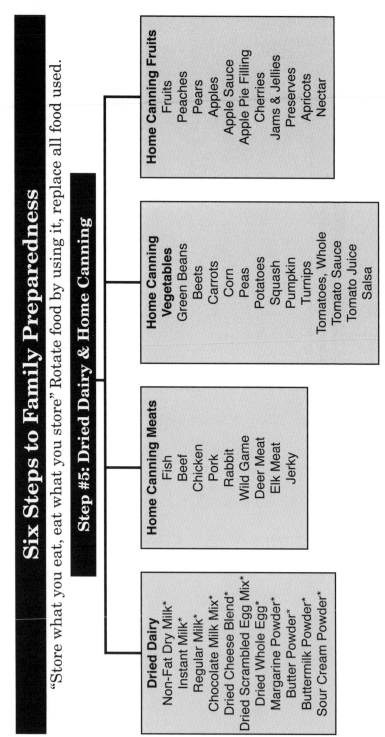

Home Canning Fruits
Fruits
Peaches
Pears
Apples
Apple Sauce
Apple Pie Filling
Cherries
Jams & Jellies
Preserves
Apricots
Nectar

Home Canning Vegetables
Green Beans
Beets
Carrots
Corn
Peas
Potatoes
Squash
Pumpkin
Turnips
Tomatoes, Whole
Tomato Sauce
Tomato Juice
Salsa

Home Canning Meats
Fish
Beef
Chicken
Pork
Rabbit
Wild Game
Deer Meat
Elk Meat
Jerky

Dried Dairy
Non-Fat Dry Milk*
Instant Milk*
Regular Milk*
Chocolate Milk Mix*
Dried Cheese Blend*
Dried Scrambled Egg Mix*
Dried Whole Egg*
Margarine Powder*
Butter Powder*
Buttermilk Powder*
Sour Cream Powder*

* Indicates availability in a #10 metal Can (approx. 1 gallon)

22

Six Steps to Family Preparedness

"Store what you eat, eat what you store" Rotate food by using it, replace all food used.

Step #6: Non-Food Items

Paper Products
Aluminum Foil
Napkins
Paper Cups
Plastic Utensils
Garbage Bags
Ziplock Baggies
Paper Plates
Paper Sacks
Paper Towels
Toilet Tissue
Waxed Paper

Cleansers
Ammonia
Bleach
Cleanser, Bath
Cleanser, Floor
Cleanser, Sink
Soap, Bath
Soap, Dish
Soap, Laundry

Hygiene
Combs
Hair Brush
Deodorant
Feminine Hygiene
Hand Lotion
Razor & blades
Tooth Brush
Tooth Paste
Shampoo
Cream Rinse
Body Soap
Makeup

Pharmacy & Medical Supplies
Adhesive Tape
Aspirin
Ibuprofen
Alcohol, Rubbing
Band Aides
Bandages
Gauze
Ointments
Vaseline
Boric Acid
Cold Remedies
Cotton & Q-Tips
Epsom Salts
First Aid Book
Iodine
Ipecac Syrup
Kaopectate
Laxatives
Milk of Magnesia
Vitamins
Personal Medication

* Indicates availability in a #10 metal Can (approx. 1 gallon)

23

Step One
First Priority

Clean out a room and make space for your grocery store and pharmacy. Organize your equipment that you have on hand and decide what equipment you need to purchase according to the chart in this book and your families needs.

Location for your Home Grocery Store

Find the coolest (temperature wise) place in the house. Usually in a basement, but preferably away from a furnace room or other heat source. If you can seal the room off so the heater vents don't heat the room, It will stay cooler. Other good locations are root cellars, insulated and heated garages, where the temperature stays constant between 40-60 degrees F. Closets, under stairways, spare bedrooms, and in an unfinished part of the house or crawl space, or under beds will work as well. North walls are cooler because they are away from the sun exposure.

If your room has dirt floors or cement, use wooden pallets to elevate the food up off the floor. The containers should never come in contact with the ground. The cans will rust and moisture can get into the buckets. Bricks with wood across them will work to elevate the food up off the floor. The air must be able to circulate around the food to keep it dry. Keep the milk, dairy products and oils closer to the floor level to keep them cooler.

Storage of grain and beans is all right in the garage because the freezing temperatures will kill bug infestation. The garage should be vented to let out the heat in the summer. The non-grain or bean items should be kept inside a room that stays between 40-60 degrees F.

Do not store food in an attic because it will get too hot and the food could parish quickly.

The room you choose should stay dry at all times. If the washer and dryer are located in this room they must be ventilated properly to prevent moisture on the food. Freezer, refrigerators, furnaces and water heaters should not be located in this room because they all give off heat, increasing the temperature.

Shelves should be designed so that a simple rotation system can effectively allow the oldest food to be used first and the newest food to be held within the shelf life period.

Seal all cracks and crevices where mice or insects might get in. Keep mouse deacon hidden in the room. Mice will ruin any unsealed buckets or cardboard containers. I have personally thrown away a lot of food because the mice have gotten into it, especially the wrapped items like yeast and MRE's (Meals Ready to Eat) or military meals. The mice eat right through the mylar foil. Keep all of these items in buckets with good sealing lids.

I have also had moth infestation. The little worm larvae eat right through the mylar also. Heavy plastic containers, jars or metal cans with tight fitting lids will keep mice and insects out. Also stick a bay leaf in with grains, flour, beans, legumes and other items to keep them from getting bug infested.

Do not leave any food items that have not been sealed properly on the shelves for any length of time. The most common insects are ants, roaches, earwigs, moths, silver fish and flour infested insects or beetles or weevils.

If any food spills, clean it up immediately. If your room becomes bug infested clean out all infested food items. Throw them away. Clean all shelves with an insecticide such as Malathion or Diazinon, spray all cracks and crevices. Do not spray it directly on food or equipment.

Never store chemicals in the same room as the food.

Shelves and Storage Areas

I have taken some pictures of food storage rooms that I feel are well planned out and organized. I hope this will give you some help on shelving ideas. I have also included plans for building a self-feeding shelving unit. You stock it from the back, the cans roll down, and you use the cans from the front. This is a way to insure proper rotation. The shelves are made so you can store camping equipment, coolers, propane stoves, sleeping blankets, etc. under them.

These shelving units have a piece of wood across the front. This keeps the bottles from falling out and breaking.

You can custom design your home grocery store and pharmacy to exactly what you need for your family.

A small board or brace across the front of your shelves keep items from rolling off (or breaking in an earthquake).

This is the same set of shelves on an adjacent wall. Note the large amount of space on the bottom to accommodate boxes, buckets, & canning equipment.

These shelves were build to accommodate home-
canned fruits, vegetables, and meats. The front-
plate on the shelves serves as a brace and keeps
the bottles from falling off.

Shelves can be built to accommodate #10 cans and still have plenty of space for five gallon buckets on the floor. The floor is a good place for coolers, dutch ovens, propane stoves, and camping supplies.

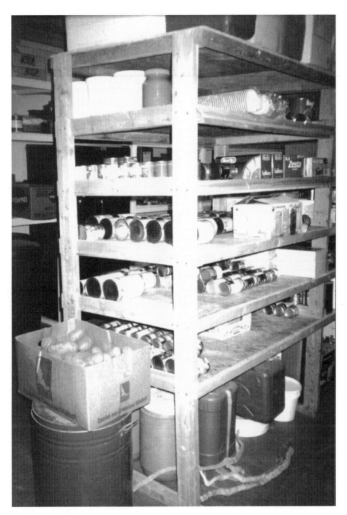

These shelves have been build to self-feed. Fill
the cans from the back and simply let them roll
forward. When you need an item, pull it from the
front and it will automatically rotate your canned
goods.

(see accompanying plans for constructing self-feeding shelves)

Basic Plans for constructing self-feeding can shelves

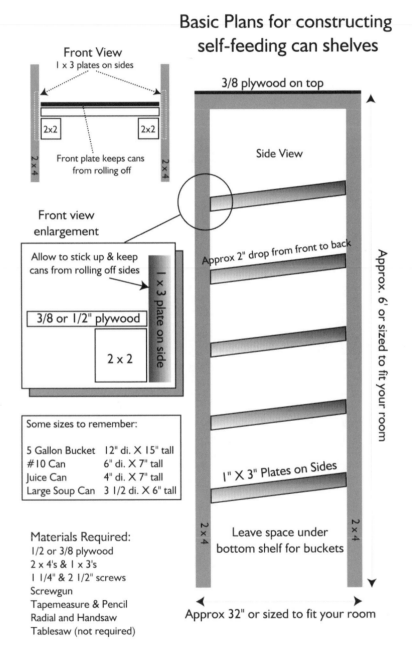

Front View
1 x 3 plates on sides

2x2   2x2

Front plate keeps cans
from rolling off

2 x 4   2 x 4

Front view enlargement

Allow to stick up & keep
cans from rolling off sides

3/8 or 1/2" plywood

1 x 3 plate on side

2 x 2

3/8 plywood on top

Side View

Approx 2" drop from front to back

Approx. 6' or sized to fit your room

1" X 3" Plates on Sides

2 x 4   2 x 4

Leave space under
bottom shelf for buckets

◀ Approx 32" or sized to fit your room ▶

Some sizes to remember:

5 Gallon Bucket	12" di. X 15" tall
#10 Can	6" di. X 7" tall
Juice Can	4" di. X 7" tall
Large Soup Can	3 1/2 di. X 6" tall

Materials Required:
1/2 or 3/8 plywood
2 x 4's & 1 x 3's
1 1/4" & 2 1/2" screws
Screwgun
Tapemeasure & Pencil
Radial and Handsaw
Tablesaw (not required)

Shelves built to accommodate buckets of bulk food.

Shelves tailor-made for water barrels, fifty pound bags of wheat, & cases of dehydrated foods. If you choose to store items on the floor put them on pallets.

Alternative Cooking and Other Equipment Needed

Make sure you have a propane stove with enough propane for three to twelve months and don't forget the matches. Store a lot of them. (Two large-boxes per month.) A wood stove is a big investment but it will come in real handy if there is no heat or power. You can cook on it as well.

Use the inventory and planning chart to check what equipment you have on hand and what you need to purchase for your program.

Water For Emergencies

Following a disaster, some people may not have access to food and water for days or weeks. Whenever there is a crisis, water is the first thing gone from the grocery store shelves. Water is even sold at very high prices to people that are desperate.

Take steps now to prepare and maintain an emergency water supply, this will prevent a difficult situation from becoming a life threatening one.

For an emergency situation a three-day supply of water is mandatory for each family member. Each person needs to drink at least one to two quarts of water per day and an additional gallon or two are required for cooking, bathing, laundry and dishes etc. If you have the room to store more water, then do so.

Children, nursing mothers and sick people may need more.

Water Storage

1. To store a large amount of water, a 55-gallon plastic polyethylene water barrel can be obtained at most food and water storage companies.
2. Water should be stored in clean and sanitary containers. Lightweight plastic containers with tight fitting lids, are the best.
3. Glass containers can break and metal containers can rust. Check the containers occasionally for leaks or cloudiness. If the water starts to look or taste bad, change it. If you have any doubts about the safety of the water to be stored, purify it before you store it. Check your water from time to time and taste it to see if it is still good. If the water goes flat, you can pour it back and forth between containers to aerate it or whipping it by hand using an eggbeater.
4. Don't over look the water supply in the hot water tank or toilet tank. Be sure to shut off the incoming water valve in case the local water supply is not safe.
5. An excellent way to store water is in two and three liter soda bottles, regular soda bottles, plastic Gatorade bottles, as well as bottled water bottles. They are heavy duty and do not break down like milk jugs. Do not use plastic milk jugs, they will leak after six months.
6. Plastic, bleach, bottles can be used by rinsing them out carefully, and filling them with water and sealing them with a tight fitting lid. It is best to use this water for doing dishes or

cleaning. It is not good to drink this water. It has too much chlorine in it.

7. To store water in glass jars, process, as you would fruit. Seal all the jars and boil pint jars for twenty minutes, quart jars for twenty-five minutes and half gallon jars for 30 minutes.

8. Tap water is good for long term storage because it is already chlorinated. If you have a clean opaque container that the light can't get through, your water should be safe. If you have any questions about whether or not your culinary water is bacteria free, purify it in some way as a precaution before you store it.

9. Some food and beverage companies that distribute syrup for soda will sell you containers. You can clean them and use them for water storage. Whatever was stored previously will leach into the water and make it taste bad, so use this water for bathing and washing dishes etc...

10. There are several sizes of containers; five gallon, fifteen gallons, and 55 gallon drums. Store several of the smaller containers because you will need to refill them from your larger container. It's important to store a 55-gallon hand pump or spigot, so you can refill the smaller ones. They are much easier to transport water in.

Water Purification

1. The safest method of purifying water is to boil it vigorously for one to three minutes. To improve the taste of the water after it has been boiled, pour the water from one container to another several times.
2. You can also purify water by adding any household bleach solution that contains 5.25 percent of sodium hypochlorite. (Most common bleach solutions contain this amount.) Add the bleach solution to the water in a clean container. Mix thoroughly by stirring or shaking. Let stand for 30 minutes. The following table shows the proper amount of 5.25 percent bleach to add to water. Do not use lemon scented or perfumed bleach.
3.

AMOUNT OF WATER	AMOUNT OF BLEACH TO ADD TO CLEAR WATER	AMOUNT OF BLEACH TO ADD TO CLOUDY WATER
1 quart-(1/4 gal.)	2 drops	4 drops
1 gallon	8 drops	16 drops
5 gallons	1/2 teaspoon	1 teaspoon

4. You can use ordinary two percent tincture of iodine, which you may have in your medicine cabinet, to purify small quantities of water. Add three drops of tincture of iodine to each quart of clear water, or six drops to each quart of cloudy water, and stir thoroughly.
5. You can safely use water purification tablets that release chlorine or iodine to purify water. They are inexpensive and you can buy them at most sporting goods stores and some drugstores.

6. A product that I really like is called ION. It is a stabilized oxygen that is very effective in killing all harmful bacteria, including giardia, cholera, and dysentery within a few minutes, and doesn't have the harmful side effects associated with Chlorine and Iodine. To use; add twenty drops of ION to one gallon of water. One bottle of ION will treat 110 gallons of water. Because ION is non-toxic it can be used medicinally and you can drink it in water to prevent illness. It can also be used topically on wounds, to kill any harmful bacteria. It's a very good item to put in your emergency medical kit. We take it with us on vacations. We put it in all liquids that are questionable. It's great for missionaries in third world countries. The shelf life of ION is indefinate. You can get ION on my website. (www.peggylayton.net)

7. I suggest that you get a hold of Mt. Olympus, Culligan, or Coca-Cola or Pepsi Cola Company and order as many cases of bottled water as you can. They come in boxes that can be stacked and if you have a business you can purchase them wholesale. We buy them for fund raisers, so I know you can get them. You can also talk to your local grocer and see if he will give you a discount if you buy a large quantity of bottled water. Make sure you get the containers that are the heavy plastic not the milk jug types. This bottled water needs to be stored in a dark, cool area to prevent bacterial growth. The milk jugs will break down and leak after about a year.

Special Diets and Personal Medications

If you are on a special diet of any type, you definitely need to take this into account in your food storage plans. Again, store what you eat and eat what you store. If you are taking medications that are mandatory to life you must store enough for at least three months.

Step Two
The Basic Ingredients for Baking

If you have the basic ingredients for baking you can make any kind of yeast bread including; white and whole-wheat bread, fry bread and scones, bagels, pita and flat breads. Also tortillas, biscuits, rolls, pancakes, waffles, cakes and frostings. Fruit crisps, pie crust, quick breads, muffins, homemade noodles, doughnuts and cooked salad dressing.

The Inventory and Planning Guide includes the items you will need to purchase for step two of this program. Work on this until it is complete, and then move to step three.

Baby Food

If you have a baby or little children, they are top priority in a crisis. Store everything you need for them including food and non-food items, such as diapers, wipes, warm blankets etc. A well-planned food storage program should allow for feeding babies and young children as well as other family members. Initially, care should be taken that the mother's diet is sufficient to permit her to nurse the infant as long as possible to provide the best source of nutrients for the baby.

It is not necessary to store large quantities of commercial baby foods. Once the infant can tolerate solid foods, he should be able to eat the foods the rest of the family is eating as long as care is taken that the foods are mashed or thinned with milk to the desired consistency.

Until the age of two, the child who is weaned from the breast needs the fats best provided by whole milk; thus it might be well to store some evaporated whole milk which could be added to the nonfat milk stored and reconstituted for the rest of the family. If the mother knows she is unable to nurse, additional whole milk sources as well as Karo syrup from which a formula could be made should be considered.

If allergies to cows milk are common to the family, the mother should consider other nutrient sources once the child is weaned. Rice gruel or other cereal base may be used in the development of a formula; sometimes-nonfat milk is tolerated whereas whole milk would not be.

Steps Three, Four, and Five
What to Store and How Much to Store

The basic food items recommended are listed below.

Grains: (300 lbs. per year per adult, 200 lbs. per child)

I recommend that you have a wide variety of grains. Do not store all wheat. Make sure your family will eat wheat. Some grains to choose from are wheat, rice, oats, corn, 6 grain and 9 grain blends, farina, germade, barley, buckwheat, rye, and super grains like: quinoa, amaranth, triticale, kamut, spelt and millet as well as all pastas such as: macaroni, spaghetti, noodles, fettuccine, and linguini.

Wheat should be less than 10% moisture content and at least 11% protein. Wheat stores better when it is in the whole-berry state. Once you crack the wheat it will not store as long.

Brown Rice:

Brown rice doesn't store very long. The outer shell of the hull contains oil. It will go rancid if it is not kept in the freezer. The shelf life is three to six months.

Legumes: (75 lbs. per person per year.)

A wide variety of beans: black beans, pinto beans, navy beans, great northern beans, small red beans, dry peas, soy beans, lentils, and sprouting seeds.

Beans are a great source of protein and when combined with rice it becomes a complete protein.

Beans can be used whole, sprouted, or ground into flour to make thickeners or refried beans. It's a great meat substitute. You can combine legumes with TVP (Textured Vegetable Protein).

Milk and Dairy Products: (50-60 lbs per person per year)
This includes non-fat powdered milk, dried eggs, cheddar cheese powder, buttermilk powder, dried butter powder and dried margarine power.

Sweeteners: (60-65 lbs. per person per year)
This includes honey, sugar, brown sugar, maple syrup, molasses, agave and stevia.

Fruits: (Dehydrated 25-30 lbs. per person per year)
This includes dried items such as apple slices, apple bits, applesauce, raisins, and fruit mix and all wet pack canned fruits.

Vegetables: (Dehydrated 40-45 lbs. per person per year)
This includes dried items such as bell peppers, broccoli, carrots, sweet corn, onions, peas, potato slices, potato dices, potato flakes, potato pearls, tomatoes, and tomato powder, and all wet pack canned vegetables.

Fats and Oils: (Two gallons of oil per person per year and twelve cans of shortening)
Dried butter and margarine powder, dried shortening powder, cooking oil, olive oil, and peanut butter are good sources for fats and oils.

Dehydrated butter, margarine, and shortening powder are also available through food storage companies.

Good quality extra virgin olive oil first run cold pressed can store for up to five years.

Meats and Meat Substitutes: (TVP or meat substitute ten to twenty pounds per person per year)

Textured vegetable protein. TVP comes in several flavors such as: beef, chicken, taco, barbecue, pepperoni, sausage, etc. Don't just store all TVP, it is ok in small amounts but contains a lot of salt and flavorings.

My personal opinion is that you need to have a wide variety of canned meats (30-50 lbs. per person.) Such as: tuna, canned salmon, and canned chicken, chunks of beef, freeze dried meats, etc.

NOTE: MSG is a terrible additive, Do not store anything with MSG in it. It makes people who are chemical sensitive very sick.

Sprouting Seeds and Beans: (10 lbs. per person per year)

Alfalfa, broccoli, radish, mung, red clover, adzuki, sunflower, garbanzo, lentils, sprouting peas, salad blends, etc. These must be specifically for sprouting. Do not nitrogen pack these seeds, it will kill them and they won't sprout. The same goes for wheat. If you plan on sprouting your wheat, label a bucket specifically for sprouting and do not nitrogen flush or put an oxygen packet in it.

Bay leaves will work well for wheat that will be used for sprouting.

Gardening Seeds: (Preferably non-hybrid)
All varieties that you like, keep your packets safe and sealed in a plastic bucket away from mice, insects and moisture.

Flavorings and Adjunct Foods:
All baking items such as baking powder, soda, yeast, salt, flavoring, spices, bouillon, soup bases, and sauces.

Psychological Foods:
Jam, jellies, drink mixes, jello, sauces, ketchup, pickles, relishes, olives, salad dressings, mayonnaise, candy, puddings, dessert filling, box mixes, popcorn, and canned juices, etc.
(fun foods).

How Much Food Do I Need For One-Year?

The following chart has recommendations for what to store and how much to store. Do not follow it exactly, use it as a guide when filling out your inventory and planning chart.

Basic & Dehydrated Foods: Suggested One Year Food Supply

The following figures are only estimates. You must determine your own nutritional needs.

Food Item	Adult		Children (ages included)				
	Male	Female	1 to 3	4 to 6	7 to 9	10 to 12	13 to 15
Wheat	200 lbs.	150 lbs.	60 lbs.	100 lbs.	150 lbs.	190 lbs.	200 lbs.
Other Grains	150 lbs.	125 lbs.	50 lbs.	60 lbs.	70 lbs.	90 lbs.	125 lbs.
Legumes	75 lbs.	50 lbs.	15 lbs.	25 lbs.	50 lbs.	60 lbs.	75 lbs.
Sweeteners	65 lbs.	60 lbs.	40 lbs.	40 lbs.	50 lbs.	60 lbs.	65 lbs.
Powdered Mild	60 lbs.	60 lbs.	80 lbs.	80 lbs.	75 lbs.	75 lbs.	75 lbs.
Dehydrated Eggs*	2 cans	2 cans	1 can	1 can	1 can	2 cans	2 cans
Salt	10 lbs.	10 lbs.	2 lbs.	5 lbs.	5 lbs.	10 lbs.	10 lbs.
Variety of Fruits* (Dehydrated)	8 cans or 25-30 lbs.	8 cans or 25-30 lbs.	4 cans or 20-25 lbs.	4 cans or 15 lbs.	6 cans or 20-25 lbs.	6 cans or 20-25 lbs.	8 cans or 25-30 lbs.
Variety of Vegetables* (Dehydrated)	15 cans or 40-45 lbs.	15 cans or 40-45 lbs.	6 cans or 15-18 lbs.	8 cans or 20-25 lbs.	10 cans or 25-30 lbs.	12 cans or 30-35 lbs.	15 cans or 40-45 lbs.
Bouillon*	1 can	1 can	1/2 can	1/2 can	1 can	1 can	1 can
Onions (Chopped)*	1 can	1 can	1/2 can	1/2 can	1 can	1 can	1 can
Cheese Powder*	2 cans	2 cans	1/2 can	1 can	2 cans	2 cans	2 cans
Tomato Powder*	2 cans	2 cans	1/2 can	1 can	2 cans	2 cans	2 cans
Oil	2 gal.	2 gal.	1 gal.	1 gal.	2 gal.	2 gal.	2 gal.
Yeast	2 lbs.	2 lbs.	1 lbs.	1 lbs.	2 lbs.	2 lbs.	2 lbs.
Sprouting Seeds	10 lbs.	10 lbs.	2 lbs.	4 lbs.	6 lbs.	10 lbs.	10 lbs.

*Indicates availability in a #10 size gallon can.

How To Store Bulk Foods
Storage Containers

Select only the best food grade containers that will exclude light, oxygen and moisture. This will greatly extend the shelf life of your food.

5 or 6-gallon plastic buckets or pails

These buckets have tight fitting lids with rubber gaskets. They are ideal for large quantities of grains, beans, legumes, sugar, flour, etc. You can purchase an inner liner that is made from a metallized foil. This liner will keep the light from harming the food and causing it to deteriorate. It also acts as a moisture barrier and keeps rodents out. The bucket with a metallized liner when sealed properly with a tight fitting lid is a very good method of storing food. To seal the mylar liner, line the bucket with the bag and fumigate with either the dry ice method or nitrogen flushing or oxygen absorber packets. See methods listed below. Then get out as much air as possible. Lay the bag flat and use an iron to heat seal the end of the bag, this way you can use the bag over and over again. Pierce a hole in the corner of the bag, hold the bag below the seal so you don't suck up the contents of the bag. Suck all the air out with the hose or a smaller attachment to the vacuum that can be inserted into the end. When the air is sucked out and the bag looks vacuum packed, hold the end and seal it with an iron. Do not let air back into the bag.

Note: Never use buckets that have contained chemicals, paint, sheet rock mud, etc. Restaurant food grade containers are ok, wash them well and rinse with bleach and water.

10 Size Double Enamel
The # 10 size cans hold approximately 1 gallon and are ideal for smaller quantities of food. You can purchase plastic lids to put on the cans after they are opened. Most food storage companies use these types of containers. They are nitrogen packed with an oxygen absorber packet sealed inside the can. These packets absorb free oxygen from the air around them and chemically bind it. This removes the oxygen from inside the can, which helps prevent insects from hatching or even living. This also prevents rancidity from occurring. The atmosphere inside the can is mostly nitrogen, which is ideal for long term storage of foods. If the oxygen level is below 2%, the food will stay good for a lot longer. If you have access to a cannery you may choose to can your own food.

Mylar Bags
The ones previously mentioned can be purchased from only food storage companies. The heaviest mylar bags in the large size are the best for lining the buckets. The bag can be sealed with a hot iron. Oxygen packets can be inserted before sealing. These bags are good gas barriers and will not allow the nitrogen or CO_2 to escape through the porous walls of the plastic.

Oxygen Absorber Packets
They look like a tea bag or sugar packet. This method is a relatively new procedure and is proving to be one of the best methods.

They must be used up within fifteen minutes of being opened and exposed to the air. These packets absorb the oxygen from the container and trap it in the iron powder, salt and moisture mixture. This is the safest way to remove oxygen. These can also be purchased from food storage companies.

The Dry Ice Method
Place about three inches of food on the bottom of the Mylar bag that is inside a plastic bucket. Then place a three-inch square of dry ice on top of the food. Fill the bucket about half full and add another piece of ice. Fill the bucket full and allow thirty minutes to two hours for the ice to dissipate. Lay the lid on loosely so the gas can escape. Then seal the bucket tightly. One pound of dry ice is used for a thirty-gallon drum of wheat. If the container bulges, take the lid off and let the gas out. Then seal it again.

CO_2 and Nitrogen Flush Method
A welding shop will rent you a Co2 tank and nitrogen gas. This can be used instead of the dry ice method. Just flush the food with the gas making sure to get the hose down into the bottom of the container after the food has been put in. Sometimes especially with flour, it can spray all over, be careful.

Bay Leaves Method
Bay leaves can be spread throughout the container. Two bay leaves for small amounts up to one gallon or five leaves in buckets. Some people say this works well for them.

Freezing Grain Method

If your buckets of grain are placed in the garage for the winter, the freezing temperatures will probably kill any weevil that is present. You can also deep freeze grain in ten-pound bags and leave it for a week to kill the bugs.

Diatomaceous Earth Method

Diatomaceous Earth can be mixed into your stored grains and beans to control insects without having to remove the dust before consuming it. For every forty pounds of grain or beans, you mix one cup of Diatomaceous Earth with it. Coat every kernel and mix it in small batches. Cover your mouth so you don't breath the dust in, it can irritate your lungs. The Diatomaceous Earth you want to use is sold as an organic garden insecticide. There are several different types of DE. Make sure you get the kind that is approved for human consumption, and not the swimming pool type.

HINT: Two liter pop bottles can be used to store grain, rice, beans, etc. for short-term usage. They stack on the shelves and you can see what is in them. Other plastic containers work also. Even ketchup and Gatorade bottles work.

The Causes of Deterioration

Oxygen
Oxygen is the one thing that will rob the nutritive value from the food. All living food contains enzymes which when exposed to oxygen start to break down the food by oxidation. The nutritive value is lost little by little as it breaks down. That is why it is very important to remove the oxygen from the containers before you package them, which I will discuss later in this section. It's also good to store grains either as a whole grain rather than a cracked grain. Once the kernel is ground the kernel dies and the rancidity process begins. Grain will store much longer in its whole grain form.

Bacteria
Bacteria, yeast and molds are controlled either by processing, canning, dehydrating, drying, freezing, etc. Bacteria is the most common cause of spoilage, so it's important to keep all food properly processed. Once beans, meat, vegetables, etc. are changed by opening and cooking them, they must be used up quickly to prevent spoilage.

Insects
Insects grow in food because the eggs or larvae are already in the product before you package it. The rodents deposit their waste product in the food and eat it as they reproduce.

Again the nitrogen pack method and oxygen absorbers will remove the oxygen and prevent insects from living. Lack of oxygen kills bugs and larvae.

51

Shelf life

Rotate your food and use it within the estimated period of time determined by research done on each product. See shelf life chart on page 56.

When the food is stored too long, two things happen:

* The nutritional value breaks down.
* The color, flavors, texture and smell changes and people will not eat it.

Light

As you find containers for your bulk food. Try to get containers that are dark and can not be permeated by light. The two most common containers that allow light in are glass jars and plastic buckets or bottles. If these are used they need to be stored in heavy cardboard boxes in a dark room.

Temperature

A cool dark place is a must. The temperature of the room should stay constant throughout the year. The lower the temperature, the longer the shelf life. The ideal temperature is (40-60 degrees F.). Most basements are between (60-70 F. degrees) and will cut the shelf life down a little. If you store your food in a garage or shed where the temperature fluctuates, you can cut the shelf life down by half the time on the chart.

Humidity and Moisture

Dehydrated foods store well when the moisture is removed. The moisture levels of dehydrated food should be under 10%. The food will be hard not leathery. Be sure to keep all containers up off the floor and away from anything that is high in humidity such as dryer vents, water heaters or anything that could flood and damage the food or rust out the cans.

Location
Find the coolest (temperature wise) place in the house. Usually in a basement, but preferably away from a furnace room or other heat source.

Dehydrated Foods

1. We use dehydrated foods everyday whether we know it or not. They are called "convenience foods." Things such as Rice-A-Roni, Hamburger Helper, Bisquick, Macaroni and Cheese, Pasta Roni, Tuna Helper, Potatoes-A-Gratin, Instant Oatmeal, instant soups like, Lipton Onion, Cup of Noodles, powdered milk, gravy mixes, and anything you "just add water" to.
2. Dehydrated foods are second only to fresh foods. They are processed under a high vacuum and low drying temperature, which removes most of the water. The product is more brittle and hard rather than leathery like dried fruits, such as raisins, figs, prunes, pineapple, apricots, and other fruits.
3. Dehydrated foods, when harvested and preserved properly will retain their vitamins, minerals and enzymes, because the food has not been cooked or canned which kills the enzymes that are so vital to the digestive process. Dehydrated food is "live food".

4. Dehydrated food is lower in weight and is much easier to store than wet pack food. It fits in cans and buckets and when reconstituted will yield at least double or triple its weight.

5. Dehydrated food is less expressive than wet pack food because you aren't paying for all the water. Food packed in #10 cans fit six cans per box and stack nicely on top of each other. If you label the boxes as to what is in them you can see at a glance what you have.

6. Dehydrated food can be rehydrated to restore it to its natural state. The taste is still great and the food value is excellent.

7. Dehydrated food stores well for long periods of time if properly canned (refer back to methods of canning) Most items keep for five to ten years.

8. Any product with powdered milk or dried eggs in it has a shorter shelf life. Rotate these items before the expiration date is up.

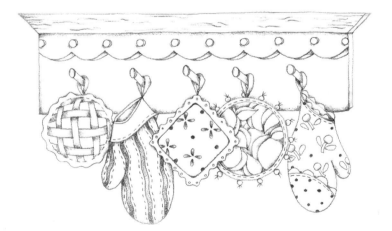

Reconstituting Guidelines

A good rule of thumb for reconstituting fruits, vegetables and meats is to add about three times the amount of boiling water to the product. Let it sit for at least twenty minutes. If cold water is used the product must sit in the refrigerator for about four hours or overnight. If you have added too much water you can drain it and use it in cooking or if it looks like it needs more water then add more.

To speed up the reconstitution process, add the dried product directly to soup and cook as usual.

When food is dehydrated the water is evaporated out and the cell walls collapse. Some products can not be reconstituted to the texture that they were before, such as tomatoes, however, they can be used in seasonings or in recipes where food is cooked. Its very easy to reconstitute food just use the reconstitution chart and "add water."

Product Reconstitution Chart

Dried Food	Shelf Life	Amount of Product	Amount of Water	Yield
Applesauce	5-7 years	1 Cup	3 Cups	3 Cups
Apple Slices	5-7 years	1 Cup	1 1/2 Cups	2 Cups
Apricot Slices	3-5 years	1 Cup	2 Cups	1 1/2 Cups
Beets	5-7 years	1 Cup	3 Cups	2 1/2 Cups
Bell Peppers	5-7 years	1 Cup	1 1/2 Cups	2 Cups
Buttermilk	3-5 years	1 Cup	1 1/2 Cups	2 1/2 Cups
Cabbage	5-7 years	1 Cup	2 1/2 Cups	2 Cups
Carrots	5-7 years	1 Cup	2 Cups	2 Cups
Celery	5-7 years	1 Cup	1 Cup	2 Cups
Cheese Sauce	3-5 years	1 Cup	1/3 Cups	2/3 Cup
Corn (Sweet)	5-7 years	1 Cup	3 Cups	2 Cups
Dates	3-5 years	1 Cup	1 Cup	1 1/3 Cups
Fruit Blend	5-7 years	1 Cup	1 1/2 Cups	1 1/2 Cups
Gelatin	5-7 years	1 Cup	4 Cups	4 Cups
Green Beans	5-7 years	1 Cup	2 Cups	2 Cups
Margarine Powder	3-5 years	1 Cup	2 tablespoons	3/4 Cup
Dehydrated Milk	3-5 years	1 Cup	4 Cups	4 Cups
Onions	5-7 years	1 Cup	1 Cup	1 1/2 Cups
Peach Slices	5-7 years	1 Cup	2 Cups	2 Cups
Peanut Butter	5-7 years	1 Cup	4 t. oil + 1/3 t. salt	1/2 Cup
Peas	5-7 years	1 Cup	2 1/2 Cups	2 1/2 Cups
Potato Dices	5-7 years	1 Cup	3 Cups	2 Cups
Potato Granules	5-7 years	1 Cup	5 Cups	5 Cups
Sour Cream	3-5 years	1 Cup	6 Tablespoons	3/4 Cup
Spinach Flakes	5-7 years	1 Cup	1 1/2 Cups	1 Cup
Tomato Powder	5-7 years	1 Cup	1 1/2 Cups	1 3/4 Cups
TVP Meat Subst.	5-7 years	1 Cup	1 Cup	1 lb. meat
Wheat & Grains	10-20 years	1 Cup	2 Cups + 1 tsp salt	3 Cups
Beans & Legumes	10 years	1 Cup	3 Cups + 2 tsp salt	3 Cups
Dehydrated Eggs	3-5 years	2 1/2 Tbsp. Egg	2 1/2 Tablespoons	1 egg
Butter Powder	3-5 years	1 Cup	2 Tablespoons	3/4 Cup
Shortening Powder	3-5 years	1 Cup	2 Tablespoons	3/4 Cup

Step Six
Nonfood Items

The Last step in this six step program is
to obtain all necessary non-food items. These
include all paper products, cleansers, personal
hygiene, medical supplies, vitamins and personal
medications. This is where the home pharmacy
comes in.

Menu Planning

It is very important to plan out two weeks
of menus and calculate all the ingredients used
for every recipe. Buy only what you know your
family will eat. These menus should all be your
favorite recipes and your family's favorite fun
foods.

When you are finished with the two weeks of
menus, then times the ingredients used by six
and that is how much you will need to store of
each item, for a three-month well rounded food
storage program.

These are the foods your family eats now.
These foods would get you by in a short-term
emergency without having to change your diet
and run the risk of getting sick.

Two Week Menu Planning Chart

These charts are to plan two weeks worth of menus and itemize all of the ingredients you'll need to purchase to have a three-month supply of the foods that you normally eat.

You must tailor your list to your families eating habits and according to the way you normally eat.

Remember:
A crisis is no time to change your diet

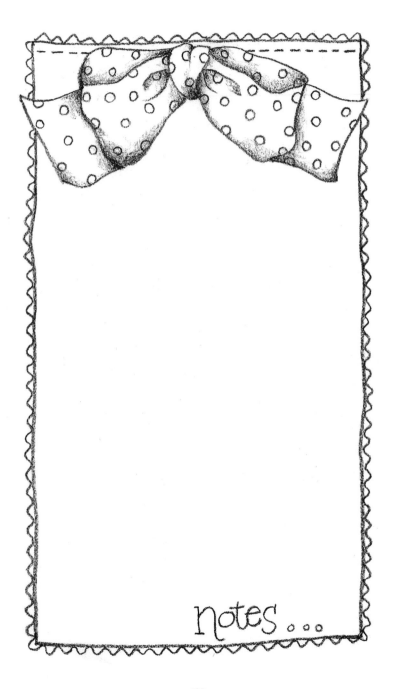

notes...

Monday

Times all ingredients by six.

Recipes Used		Ingredients Required
Breakfast		
Lunch		
Dinner		

Tuesday

Times all ingredients by six.

Recipes Used	Ingredients Required

Breakfast

Lunch

Dinner

Wednesday

Times all ingredients by six.

Recipes Used	Ingredients Required
Breakfast	
Lunch	
Dinner	

Thursday

Times all ingredients by six.

Recipes Used	Ingredients Required
Breakfast	
Lunch	
Dinner	

Friday

Times all ingredients by six.

Recipes Used	Ingredients Required
Breakfast	
Lunch	
Dinner	

Saturday

Times all ingredients by six.

Recipes Used	Ingredients Required
Breakfast	
Lunch	
Dinner	

Sunday

Times all ingredients by six.

Recipes Used	Ingredients Required
Breakfast	
Lunch	
Dinner	

Monday

Times all ingredients by six.

Recipes Used	Ingredients Required
Breakfast	
Lunch	
Dinner	

Tuesday

Times all ingredients by six.

Recipes Used	Ingredients Required
Breakfast	
Lunch	
Dinner	

Wednesday

Times all ingredients by six.

Recipes Used	Ingredients Required

Breakfast

Lunch

Dinner

Thursday

Times all ingredients by six.

Recipes Used		Ingredients Required
Breakfast		
Lunch		
Dinner		

Friday

Times all ingredients by six.

Recipes Used	Ingredients Required
Breakfast	
Lunch	
Dinner	

Saturday

Times all ingredients by six.

Recipes Used	Ingredients Required
Breakfast	
Lunch	
Dinner	

Sunday

Times all ingredients by six.

Recipes Used	Ingredients Required
Breakfast	
Lunch	
Dinner	

Itemized Weekly Ingredients

This chart is to itemize all of the ingredients needed for the previous two week menu plan. Times all ingredients by six to come up with a three month inventory of items you use on a regular basis.

Family Name: _____ # in Family _____

Item	Amt. Required by Family	Amount On Hand	Amount Needed

Item	Amt. Required by Family	Amount On Hand	Amount Needed

Rotation of Food

Many families or individuals desire to maintain a one-year supply of food. This has become a way of life for some. Most food systems involve growing and preserving food at home from gardens and orchards, or purchasing fruit and vegetables in season and "putting up" or canning these foods.

Although some items may keep for a long time, every item needs to be rotated so that it is used up and replenished within one to three years.

Many of the dehydrated products are prone to deterioration if they are kept for more than five to seven years.

Rotating canned goods as well as dehydrated food will assure better quality and nutritive value.

When rotating food, use the oldest dated food first. Put the newest food purchased to the back and pull from the front as you use the food. This is how the grocery stores do it so food doesn't get old on the shelves.

Meat supplies are most often obtained in the fall and winter months, when the wild game season in on. Lots of families raise beef, pork, chickens, etc. and slaughter them during the cooler months.

Most people stock up on food during harvest in the fall and early winter. If you took a poll of how many families are prepared with a six to twelve month supply of food. You would find them more prepared in the late fall, early winter than in the spring and summer. It is a natural thing to stock up with food as winter approaches, then to deplete it through the winter and spring.

Inventory and Planning Guide

The next step is to take inventory and plan your food storage program.

This inventory-planning guide has been prepared to assist you in accessing your individual family preparedness needs.

It is very important that you are very accurate in knowing what items you have on hand. The more accurate you are in your planning the easier it will be to complete your program.

Planning Your Food Storage Program

1. Food storage should be well planned out and purchased in a systematic and orderly fashion to avoid panic buying.
2. Borrowing money or putting the purchase on a credit card without means to pay it back is highly discouraged.
3. Budgeting and shopping wisely when items are on sale will save you a lot of money.
4. Only buy what you know your family will eat or it will be money wasted.
5. Food should be rotated and replaced on a regular basis each time you use an item.
6. Keep your food inventory list handy and mark the items as you use them so they can be replaced.
7. Use a marker to mark what each item is, when it was purchased and when it needs to be used.

Instructions

1. Make your two-week menu plan of meals that you are use to cooking and your family likes. Copy the menu planning charts, tape them to the refrigerator and keep track of everything your family eats for two weeks. It is important to list each and every ingredient in all the recipes. This will help you calculate the amount of food your family eats under normal circumstances. Then times all these ingredients by six to get a well-rounded three-month list of ingredients to purchase from the store. This list is for the entire family. "Remember these are your buffer foods" they will get you by for a short term crises without having to change your families diet. This will help reduce the risk of illness due to change in diet. As we discussed before, little children and older people have a harder time adjusting to the basics; wheat, beans, honey and powdered milk. However the whole family will be sick if you change the diet drastically.
2. Study your inventory-planning guide carefully. Using the different categories for food and non-food items.
3. Choose the appropriate sections for the foods you are taking inventory of.
4. Using a separate piece of paper if necessary count all case goods, dehydrated food cans and containers and estimate approximately how much is in each can or bucket. Go through your entire house, garage, basement, and anywhere else you might have stashed food and non-food items. (This is going to be a very time

consuming job. Take a whole week if necessary to do this. It's the most important thing to do first.)

5. Determine the amounts needed and the number of people in the family and to the best of your ability, estimate what you need for three months as well as one year. Subtract what you have on hand and determine what you need to purchase.

6. It is very expensive to purchase a years supply of one item, so take it three months at a time. When that is complete take a yellow high-lighter and highlight that item to show that you have completed it. Again a three-month well-rounded supply of food and non-food items is much better than a years supply of wheat, beans, honey and powdered milk. We will not be able to tolerate a diet of dehydrated food, wheat and beans etc... without supplementing it with all the other foods that you normally eat.

7. Complete the above steps for every item you feel you can not live without and desire to have in your preparedness program.

8. If you have any item that is not on the inventory list write it down under "other" at the bottom of the product column. If you need more space, attach another piece of paper to your planning guide.

9. Remember... this is your personal program. Every family must have their own grocery store. Everyone's needs are different. Don't use your parents, sisters, brothers, or neighbor's lists. Select only those products your family eats now and introduce slowly the products

they are not use to eating. The old wives tale "If your hungry enough you'll eat anything" just isn't true.

Good Luck and may God bless you as you go about getting your house in order.

Inventory and Planing Chart for a Basic and Balanced Food Storage Plan

All Recommendations are for 1 person

Step One: Alternative Cooking Methods and Other Equipment

Dutch Ovens						
Propane Cook Stove						
Extra Propane						
Wood Burning Stove						
3 Mos. Supply/Wood						
Metal grate or screen for Fire						
Matches (12 Boxes)						
Electric Grain Mill						
Hand Grain Mill						
Garden Seeds						
Water Containers						
Water Purifier						
Buckets & Lids						
Sprouting Equipment						
Dehydrator						
Blender						
Mixer						
Vacuum Sealer						
Juicer						
Canning Equipment						
Jars, Lids. Rings, etc.						
Water Bath Canner						
Pressure Cooker						
Bucket Openers						
Can Openers						

Step One: Water & Mandatory Medications

One gal. per person per day. 90 Gallon Minimum (three mos. supply)

Water			
Purification Tablets			
ION Water Purification			
Medications			

Step Two: Basic Baking Ingredients

Basic Baking Ingredients	Amount on Hand	Individual Amt. for 3 Mo.	Individual Amt. for 1 Year	# of People in Family	3 Months for Entire Family	1 Year for Family
Wheat For Grinding						
White Flour*						
Powdered Milk*						
Dried Whole Egg*						
Baking Soda						
Salt						
Baking Powder						
Corn Starch						
Yeast						
Sweeteners						
White Sugar						
Brown Sugar						
Powdered Sugar						
Honey						
Molasses						
Corn Syrup						
Maple Syrup						

•Indicates availability in a #10 metal can (approx. I gallon)

Step Two: Basic Baking Ingredients (continued)

Basic Baking Ingredients	Amount on Hand	Individual Amt. for 3 Mo.	Individual Amt. for 1 Year	# of People in Family	3 Months for Entire Family	1 Year for Family
Fats						
Shortening						
Oil						
Butter Powder*						
Margarine Powder*						
Shortening Powder*						
Spices/Flavorings						
Baking Cocoa						
Cinnamon						
Nutmeg						
Vanilla						
Powdered Lemon						
Lemon Juice						
Oats*						
Cornmeal*						
Buttermilk Powder*						
Dried Fruit						
Apple Sauce*						
Apple Slices*						
Bananas*						
Fruit Blend*						
Raisins						
Chocolate Chips						

Step Two: Baby Supplies

Baby Supplies	Amount on Hand	Individual Amt. for 3 Mo.	Individual Amt. for 1 Year	# of People in Family	3 Months for Entire Family	1 Year for Family
Baby Food						
Formula						
Baby Cereal						
Evaporated Milk						
Karo Syrup						
Canned Baby Food						
Diapers & Pins						
Baby Wipes						
Rash Ointment						
Baby Bath						
Lotion						
Shampoo						
Baby Medication						

Step Three: Grains, Cereals, Pastas, Legumes, Beans & Spices

Basic Grains	Amount on Hand	Individual Amt. for 3 Mo.	Individual Amt. for 1 Year	# of People in Family	3 Months for Entire Family	1 Year for Family
Wheat. Red*						
Wheat, White*						
Wheat Grinder						
Rye						
Rice. White						
Rice, Brown						
Barley*						
Oats. Instant*						
Oat Groats, Whole*						
Corn Meal*						
Whole Corn*						
Pancake Mix*						
White Flour						
Triticale						
Amaranth						
Quinoa						
Kamut						
Spelt						

•Indicates availability in a #10 metal can (approx. I gallon)

Step Three: Cereals & Rice

Cereals & Rice	Amount on Hand	Individual Amt. for 3 Mo.	Individual Amt. for 1 Year	# of People in Family	3 Months for Entire Family	1 Year for Family
Cereals						
Cracked Wheat*						
Millet*						
Cream of Wheat*						
Farina*						
Granola*						
Oatmeal*						
Brown Rice						
White Rice*						

Step Three: Pastas

Pastas	Amount on Hand	Individual Amt. for 3 Mo.	Individual Amt. for 1 Year	# of People in Family	3 Months for Entire Family	1 Year for Family
Macaroni, Elbow*						
Macaroni, Shells*						
Spaghetti*						
Egg Noodles*						
Lasagna						
Fettuccine						
Linguini						

•Indicates availability in a #10 metal can (approx. 1 gallon)

Step Three: Legumes

Legumes	Amount on Hand	Individual Amt. for 3 Mo.	Individual Amt. for 1 Year	# of People in Family	3 Months for Entire Family	1 Year for Family
Lentils*						
Split Peas*						
Yellow Peas*						
Whole Peas*						

Step Three: Beans

Beans	Amount on Hand	Individual Amt. for 3 Mo.	Individual Amt. for 1 Year	# of People in Family	3 Months for Entire Family	1 Year for Family
Lima, Large*						
Lima, Baby*						
Mung*						
Small White Navy*						
Pinto*						
Small Red*						
Soy*						
Kidney*						
Black Turtle*						
Pink*						

•Indicates availability in a #10 metal can (approx. I gallon)

Step Three: Sprouting Seeds

Sprouting Seeds	Amount on Hand	Individual Amt. for 3 Mo.	Individual Amt. for 1 Year	# of People in Family	3 Months for Entire Family	1 Year for Family
Alfalfa Seeds						
Red Clover						
Broccoli Seeds						
Radish Seeds						
Pumpkin Seeds						
Sunflower Seeds						
Salad Mix Seeds						
Garbanzos or Chick Peas						
Barley						
Lentils						
Mung Beans						
Soy Beans						
Wheat						

•Indicates availability in a #10 metal can (approx. I gallon)

Step Three: Spices

Spices	Amount on Hand	Individual Amt. for 3 Mo.	Individual Amt. for 1 Year	# of People in Family	3 Months for Entire Family	1 Year for Family
Allspice, Ground						
Apple Pie Spice						
Bacon Bits						
Barbecue Spice						
Basil Leaves						
Bay Leaves						
Cilantro Flakes						
Celery Flakes						
Cinnamon, Ground						
Cinnamon Sticks						
Chili Powder						
Cloves, Whole						
Cloves, Ground						
Cream of Tartar						
Cumin, Ground						
Dill Seed						
Dill Weed						
Garlic Powder						
Garlic Salt						
Ginger, Ground						
Italian Seasoning						
Lemon Pepper						
Mustard, Ground						
Nutmeg, Ground						
Onion, Minced						
Onion Salt						

89

Step Three: Spices

Spices	Amount on Hand	Individual Amt. for 3 Mo.	Individual Amt. for 1 Year	# of People in Family	3 Months for Entire Family	1 Year for Family
Oregano Leaves						
Oregano, Ground						
Paprika						
Parsley Flakes						
Pickling Spice						
Poppy Seeds						
Poultry Seasoning						
Pepper, Black						
Peppercorns						
Pepper, White						
Pepper, Cayenne						
Pumpkin Pie Spice						
Sage, Rubbed						
Sesame Seeds						
Seasoning Salt						
Taco Seasoning						
Thyme, Ground						

•Indicates availability in a # 10 metal can (approx. 1 gallon)

Step Three: Commercial Soups					
Commercial Soups	Amount on Hand	Individual Amt. for 3 Mo.	Individual Amt. for 1 Year	# of People in Family	3 Months for Entire Family	1 Year for Family
Bean & Bacon						
Cream of Chicken						
Cream of Mushroom						
Celery						
Chicken Noodle						
Clam Chowder						
Consomme						
Potato						
Vegetable						
Vegetable Beef						

Step Three: Dehydrated Soups, Sauces & Spice Mixes

Soups, Sauces & Spice Mixes	Amount on Hand	Individual Amt. for 3 Mo.	Individual Amt. for 1 Year	# of People in Family	3 Months for Entire Family	1 Year for Family
ABC Soup Mix*						
Veg. Stew Blend*						
Cream Soup Base*						
Cheese Blend*						
Chili Seasoning						
Gravy Mixes						
Taco Seasoning						
Spaghetti Seasoning						
Tomato Powder*						
Beef Bouillon*						
Chicken Bouillon*						
Corn Soup						
Mushroom Soup						
Onion Soup						
Split Pea Soup						

•Indicates availability in a #10 metal can (approx. 1 gallon)

92

Step Four: Meats & Other Protein Foods

Protein Foods	Amount on Hand	Individual Amt. for 3 Mo.	Individual Amt. for 1 Year	# of People in Family	3 Months for Entire Family	1 Year for Family
Tuna Fish						
Canned Salmon						
Spam						
Beef Dices						
Beef Jerky						
Beef & Rice						
Beef Stroganoff						
Beef Steak						
Beef Stew						
Chicken Chop Suey						
Chicken Dices						
Chicken Stew						
Chili Mac with Beef						
Ham Dices						
Sausage Patties						
Bacon Bits TVP*						
Dried Egg Mix*						
Dried Whole Eggs*						
Peanut Butter Powder*						
Peanut Butter						

•Indicates availability in a #10 metal can (approx. l gallon)

Step Four: Meat, Meat Substitutes & Other Protein Foods

Protein Foods	Amount on Hand	Individual Amt. for 3 Mo.	Individual Amt. for 1 Year	# of People in Family	3 Months for Entire Family	1 Year for Family
Beef Chunks TVP*						
Chicken TVP*						
Ham TVP *						
Plain TVP*						
Taco TVP *						
Barbecue TVP*						
Sausage TVP *						
Pepperoni TVP *						
Sloppy Joe TVP*						
Pork TVP*						
Clams						
Corned Beef						
Roast Beef (canned)						
Ham (canned)						
Shrimp (canned)						
Spam						
Kipper Snacks						

•Indicates availability in a #10 metal can (approx. I gallon)

Step Four: Psychological Foods

Psychological Foods	Amount on Hand	Individual Amt. for 3 Mo.	Individual Amt. for 1 Year	# of People in Family	3 Months for Entire Family	1 Year for Family
Hot Chocolate Mix*						
Lemonade*						
Orange Drink Mix*						
Tropical Punch*						
Apple Juice						
Apricot Juice						
Carrot Juice						
Orange Juice						
Pineapple Juice						
Tomato Juice						
Gelatin, all flavors*						
Puddings*						
Tapioca						
Dessert Fillings						
Popcorn*						
Ketchup						
Mayonnaise						
Mustard						
Salad Dressing						
Hot Peppers						
Dill Pickles						
Olives						
Relishs						
Sauces						

•Indicates availability in a #10 metal can (approx. I gallon)

Step Five: Commercial Fruits

Commercial Fruits	Amount on Hand	Individual Amt. for 3 Mo.	Individual Amt. for 1 Year	# of People in Family	3 Months for Entire Family	1 Year for Family
Applesauce						
Apple Pie Filling						
Apricots						
Blueberries						
Cherries						
Cherry Pie Filling						
Fruit Cocktail						
Mandarin Oranges						
Peaches						
Pears						
Pineapple						
Plums						

•Indicates availability in a #10 metal can (approx. 1 gallon)

Step Five: Dehydrated Fruits

Dehydrated Fruits	Amount on Hand	Individual Amt. for 3 Mo.	Individual Amt. for 1 Year	# of People in Family	3 Months for Entire Family	1 Year for Family
Apple Slices*						
Apple Sauce*						
Apricots						
Banana Slices*						
Fruit Blend*						
Peach/Apple Flakes*						
Strawberry/Apple Flakes*						
Prunes						
Raisins*						
Dates						
Figs						

•Indicates availability in a #10 metal can (approx. I gallon)

Step Five: Commercial Wet Pack Vegetables

Wet Pack Vegetables	Amount on Hand	Individual Amt. for 3 Mo.	Individual Amt. for 1 Year	# of People in Family	3 Months for Entire Family	1 Year for Family
Asparagus						
Beans, Green						
Beans, Kidney						
Beans, Pinto						
Pork and Beans						
Carrots						
Corn, Whole						
Corn. Creamed						
Mushrooms						
Peas, Sweet Garden						
Potatoes						
Tomatoes, Stewed						
Tomatoes. Whole						
Vegetables, Mixed						

98

Step Five: Dehydrated Vegetables

Dehydrated Vegetables	Amount on Hand	Individual Amt. for 3 Mo.	Individual Amt. for 1 Year	# of People in Family	3 Months for Entire Family	1 Year for Family
Bell Peppers*						
Broccoli Florettes*						
Carrot Dices*						
Cabbage*						
Celery*						
Onions, Chopped*						
Mushrooms, Dried*						
Peas, Sweet*						
Green Beans*						
Corn, Sweet Kernel*						
Vegetable Stew*						
Tomato Powder*						
Potato Dices*						
Potato Flakes*						
Potato Granules*						
Potato Pearls*						

•Indicates availability in a #10 metal can (approx. I gallon)

Step Five: Dehydrated Dairy & Egg Products

Dehydrated Dairy Products	Amount on Hand	Individual Amt. for 3 Mo.	Individual Amt. for 1 Year	# of People in Family	3 Months for Entire Family	1 Year for Family
Non-Fat dry Milk*						
Instant dry Milk*						
Regular dry Milk*						
Chocolate Milk*						
Cheese Blend*						
Dried Egg Mix Scrambled*						
Dried Whole Egg*						
Margarine Powder*						
Butter Powder*						
Buttermilk Powder*						
Sour Cream Powder						

*Indicates availability in a #10 metal can (approx. 1 gallon)

Step Five: Home Canning and Preservation

Canning Products	Amount on Hand	Individual Amt. for 3 Mo.	Individual Amt. for 1 Year	# of People in Family	3 Months for Entire Family	1 Year for Family
Green Beans						
Beets						
Carrots						
Corn						
Peas						
Potatoes						
Squash						
Pumpkin						
Turnips						
Tomatoes, Whole						
Tomato Sauce						
Tomato Juice						
Salsa						
Canned Meats						
Fruits						
Peaches						
Pears						
Apples						
Apple Sauce						
Apple Pie Filling						
Cherries						
Jams & Jellies						
Preserves						
Apricots						
Nectar						
Pickles						

Step Six: Non-Food Items & Paper Goods

Non-Food Items	Amount on Hand	Individual Amt. for 3 Mo.	Individual Amt. for 1 Year	# of People in Family	3 Months for Entire Family	1 Year for Family
Aluminum Foil						
Napkins						
Paper Cups						
Plastic Utensils						
Garbage Baas						
Ziplock Baggies						
Paper Plates						
Paper Sacks						
Paper Towels						
Toilet Tissue						
Waxed Paper						

Step Six: Cleansers

Cleansers	Amount on Hand	Individual Amt. for 3 Mo.	Individual Amt. for 1 Year	# of People in Family	3 Months for Entire Family	1 Year for Family
Ammonia						
Bleach						
Cleanser, Bath						
Cleanser, Floor						
Cleanser, Sink						
Soap, Bath						
Soap, Dish						
Soap, Laundry						

Step Six: Personal Hygiene

Personal Hygiene	Amount on Hand	Individual Amt. for 3 Mo.	Individual Amt. for 1 Year	# of People in Family	3 Months for Entire Family	1 Year for Family
Combs						
Hair Brush						
Deodorant						
Feminine Hygiene						
Hand Lotion						
Razor						
Razor Blades						
Tooth Brush						
Tooth Paste						
Shampoo						
Cream Rinse						
Body Soap						
Makeup						

Step Six: Medical Supplies

Medical Supplies	Amount on Hand	Individual Amt. for 3 Mo.	Individual Amt. for 1 Year	# of People in Family	3 Months for Entire Family	1 Year for Family
Adhesive Tape						
Aspirin						
Ibuprofen						
Alcohol, Rubbing						
Band Aides						
Bandages						
Gauze						
Ointments						
Vaseline						
Boric Acid						
Cold Remedies						
Cotton & Q-Tips						
Epsom Salts						
First Aid Book						
First Aid Kit						
Hot Water Bottle						
Iodine						
Ipecac Syrup						
Kaopectate						
Laxatives						
Milk of Magnesia						
Vitamins						
Personal Medication						

Step Six: Personalized Family Pharmacy

Medical Supplies	Amount on Hand	Individual Amt. for 3 Mo.	Individual Amt. for 1 Year	# of People in Family	3 Months for Entire Family	1 Year for Family
Personal Medication						
Personal Vitamins						
Vitamin C						
Calcium						

Products Available Through Mail Order:

Books

Food Storage 101 Where Do I Begin? $ 12.95
Emergency Food Storage and
    Survival Handbook $ 15.95
Cookin' with Home Storage $ 14.95
Cookin' with Dried Eggs $ 7.50
Cookin' with Powdered Milk $ 9.50
Cookin' with Rice and Beans $ 12.95
Cookin' with Potatoes $ 12.95
Cookin' with Kids in the Kitchen $ 12.95

Upcoming Books Available Soon

Cookin' with Wheat and Other Grains
You Can Live On Soup and Bread
Cookin' with Dehydrated Foods
Copy Cat Cookin' (Make your own Boxed
    mixes, like Hamburger Helper, Rice-a-Roni,
    Oatmeal packets, and, lots, more)
Great Grandma' Recipes, Remedies, &
    Washday Hints

Dehydrated Foods Available

If you can not find dehydrated foods locally, you can write to me for sources and price lists available through mail order.

*All foods are packaged in gallon (#10 can) containers or 5 gallon buckets.

ION (water purification) 110 gal. Treatment
$14.95
To purchase **ION** check my website:
www.peggylayton.net

For current prices of these and other food storage products, write to:

Peggy Layton
P.O. Box 44
Manti, UT 84642
(435) 835-0311 or (435) 851-0777
www.peggylayton.net

Name: _____

Address: _____

City: State: _____

Zip: _____ Phone: _____

Please send me the following books.

_____

_____

_____

_____

_____

_____

Or list selections on a separate sheet of paper. Enclose tax (Utah residents add 6.25%) and $3.95 shipping for the first book and $1.00 for each additional book.

Total Amount Enclosed $ _____

Group Rates & Wholesale Pricing Available.
Check website for prices.